A MAN NAMED
BRANCH

THE TRUE STORY OF BASEBALL'S
GREAT EXPERIMENT

MARJORIE MADDOX

Loch Ness
Books

an imprint of Sunbury Press, Inc.
Mechanicsburg, PA USA

Loch Ness
Books

an imprint of Sunbury Press, Inc.
Mechanicsburg, PA USA

For information about special discounts for bulk purchases, please contact Sunbury Press Orders Dept. at (855) 338-8359 or orders@sunburypress.com.

To request one of our authors for speaking engagements or book signings, please contact Sunbury Press Publicity Dept. at publicity@sunburypress.com.

FIRST LOCH NESS PRESS EDITION: January 2026

Set in Adobe Garamond Pro | Interior design by Crystal Devine | Cover by Darlene Sedjro | Edited by Anaya Montgomery.

Publisher's Cataloging-in-Publication Data
Names: Maddox, Marjorie, author.
Title: A man named Branch : the true story of baseball's great experiment / Marjorie Maddox.
Description: First trade paperback edition. | Mechanicsburg, PA : Loch Ness Press, 2026.
Summary: In 1947, Jackie Robinson changed history. But who thought of this idea? *A Man Named Branch: The True Story of Baseball's Great Experiment* explains, through narrative nonfiction, how a farm boy from Duck Run, Ohio, kept ideas "brewing in his brain" that led to baseball's integration and eventually helped pave the way for the Civil Rights Movement.
Identifiers: ISBN : 979-8-88819-341-9 (paperback).
Subjects: BIOGRAPHY & AUTOBIOGRAPHY / Sports | SPORTS & RECREATION / Baseball / History | YOUNG ADULT NONFICTION / Biography & Autobiography / Sports & Recreation.

Designed in the USA
0 1 1 2 3 5 8 13 21 34 55

For the Love of Books!

To Great Uncle Branch (1881–1965),
and to my mother (1929–2021), who kept the stories alive.

CONTENTS

1

When Money Was Tight and Families Tighter

His name was Branch, and in his brain was brewing a great experiment.

Just like you, just like me, he started off as a kid. He started off as a kid in Duck Run, Ohio.

"Duck Run," you say?

Yes, Duck Run, a tiny little town no bigger than your thumb on a map of the state that's round on the ends and high in the middle: O-Hi-O.

And ducks?

Ducks and farms and, in nearby Turkey Creek, a one-room schoolhouse where, in 1898, Branch taught a whole room of kids when he was only seventeen.

Before that, he was just a poor boy who stuttered, spitting out letters that stuck on his tongue, practicing until patience polished his speech.

He was a poor boy who devoured any book he could find, like the waterlogged ones his father brought home from fire sales: books by Washington Irving and Dante, stories glowing with adventure.

He had ideas, that boy Branch. They were always bubbling in his brain. He experimented with this and that, taking risks, seeing which choice was stronger, wiser, and—most of all—the right thing to do.

He had ideas and wanted to help when the going got tough. In the mid-1890s, the going was always tough in small-town Ohio. Crops to save, mouths to feed, and relatives to help. He was young, strong, and needed on the farm. Money was tight and families tighter. Family was important to Branch. Oh yes, family was incredibly important.

There was big brother Orla, away at teaching, who worshipped baseball and taught Branch to pitch and catch.

There was little brother Frank, who worshipped Branch, and grew up to catch bootleggers and scout baseball.

There was his mother, who later made him promise, "Sunday is for the pew, not the ballpark"—a promise he always kept.

There was his father, who sowed corn, sorghum, and salvation. He taught his son the merit of hard work: feeding cattle, hogs, and hungry souls.

And so, Branch prayed and plowed. He slopped pigs. He lifted hay and hymns high to his Lord. And all the while, in his brain was brewing a great experiment.

Ideas were brewing—ideas of daring and courage. They kept percolating. Branch wanted to teach like his big brother. Like Orla, he lived to play this new game of baseball with a joy so glorious that some days it swept him away.

He had ideas but no fancy diploma, no high school certificate with a pretty gold stamp, just big biceps from working the farm. That was enough for Branch.

He did it all on his own: read and studied and worked the farm and then read and studied and worked the farm some more and—with his parents' okay—became a teacher, a teacher at that one-room schoolhouse.

2

Standing Ground

Now, lots of teachers had been in the Turkey Creek one-room school-house before. Most of them had hightailed it. That tiny school had some of the meanest bullies around, roughnecks who even bullied the teachers. They spat tobacco juice at more than a couple and beat up another few until the teachers were bruised and bloody. Can you imagine?

When a bully challenged Branch, he didn't back down. Not Branch. Strong from the farm, he stood his ground—and won. Because it was the right thing to do. Because you can't let bullies rule your life. Because *all* of the students deserved their chance to learn to fight with their brains too.

For this, the whole town loved him, signed a petition, and voted for him to stay and teach forever—well, at least for two years. But his name was Branch, and in his brain was brewing a great experiment.

What would he do?

He wanted to marry his sweetheart, but his job was not good enough in her father's eyes. He wanted to go to college but had no bank account large enough—and no wealthy father either. (In those days, mostly rich kids went to college, not a poor farm boy like Branch, who didn't even have a high school diploma.) And, he wanted to play ball. Oh, how he wanted to play ball!

His brain was almost bursting with decisions, with this choice and that one battling for attention. He didn't forget his family either or his sweetheart Jennie Moulton, who later went by Jane. He talked with them all.

He thought, talked, prayed. He would finish the experiment of teaching he started in that one-room schoolhouse. He would have patience and finish his commitment. Then he would go to college at nearby Ohio Wesleyan University. First, he would have to study Latin, and more math, but he would do it. That was the right thing to do. That was who he was.

In 1901, Branch's nervous parents waved goodbye. They were afraid of the worldly ways of universities but confident in the integrity of their son. And, Jennie, well, she was confident too, and sent Branch off with a kiss to his new college experiment: classes, sports, and odd jobs, as many as he could juggle.

One of those jobs was playing catcher for the semi-pro Portsmouth Navies—close to home and with a better paycheck than he earned

Branch Rickey as a student at Ohio Wesleyan University, 1903

4

from heaving hay! Branch thought he hit a home run. He was round-ing the bases.

But sometimes even with the best intentions, inexperience tags you out. Branch learned this soon enough. The next fall, the college president called him in to say, "No paid athletes allowed at the college!" Talk about a tense moment! It had never occurred to Branch that he wasn't allowed to play baseball at Ohio Wesleyan while getting paid to play outside of the college too.

Ideas were sure brewing in his brain then: ideas about losing every-thing and starting over, ideas about embarrassing his family and his girl. No more college varsity position; maybe no more school at all! The owner of the Portsmouth Navies even swore to the college that Branch never got a penny. That was a lie, and Branch would have none of that.

No, he had to take a stand.

It was risky but right. Sometimes folks don't notice when you make the right choice, but you need to make it anyway. Sometimes folks do notice. This time, at least one person did.

Despite being called out, Branch discovered that the game changed. Some changes were good. Sure, he couldn't catch for the college varsity team now, but he wasn't kicked out of school either. The president was too impressed with him for that. Even better, Branch got the okay to play professional baseball *and* football for area teams. He got to play his sports *and* get paid! Now that was a nice surprise. It meant he could pay his bills and keep learning—he always wanted to keep learning. Eventually, he could even marry his sweetheart.

A year and a few broken bones later, Branch was done with football, but oh how everything took off in baseball. Everything took off, but not in the way Branch expected. Not in the way anyone expected.

Sometimes you look back on something in your life and realize only later how important it was. That's what happened here. What came next was the start of something big, the small seed of an idea that turned into Branch's great experiment. Sometimes that's how the best ideas start. They are sown early, and much, much later, they bloom. In this case, the idea that was sown turned into breaking baseball's color barrier. But Branch didn't know that until later, much later.

3

Another Town, Another Bully

Here's what happened. Here's how something sad turned into an idea that eventually turned into something great—the "Great Experiment," in fact.

When the college lost its baseball coach, Branch was hired in his place. He loved coaching, but boy, did he get tired of one thing: the bullying. This bullying was even worse than at that one-room schoolhouse in Turkey Creek. Here, rival players were picking on his first baseman, Charles "Tommy" Thomas, one of the few African Americans at the school and the only one on the team. Now, Tommy wanted to be a dentist, but he sure was handy with a bat and ball. That didn't stop opponents from hurling insults. In 1903, one Kentucky coach even pulled all of his players from a game with Ohio Wesleyan. No way was that coach going to let his players on the same field as black Tommy!

Branch didn't like that at all. He didn't use his fists like at that one-room schoolhouse, but he sure raised his voice. He argued and yelled and argued and yelled. Finally, just like at Turkey Creek, he won. Tommy took the field with everyone else.

The problems didn't stop there. This was the early 1900s, and there was more than plenty of ugliness to go around. Racial slurs. Violence. Segregation at its height, with bullies saying who could enter through which door, drink from which water fountain, eat at which restaurant, and sleep in which hotel. It wasn't stopping any time soon—not for another sixty years.

6

Charles "Tommy" Thomas (center back row) and Branch Rickey (far right, back row) on the 1904 Ohio Wesleyan baseball team

The next baseball season, when Branch's team was traveling in Indiana, problems kept mounting. "No way," a hotel clerk said in his not-so-nice tone, "No way *that boy's* staying. This here's a whites-only establishment." Another town, another bully.

But Branch was Branch. He was thinking about what was right. He was thinking about strategy. Now he was thinking even more about the power of words instead of the power of fists.

Branch bought some time. He was crafty and smart. He sent someone out to check for rooms at the YMCA and in black neighborhoods. Then he used his sweet-talking tongue once again. Pretty soon, Branch was convincing the manager to let Tommy wait in Branch's room. But that wasn't the end.

His name was Branch, and in his brain . . .

Pretty soon, Branch arranged for a cot to be sent up.

. . . was brewing a great experiment.

Pretty soon the manager was livid.

His name was Branch, and in his brain . . .

And Branch was livid right back.

. . . was brewing a great experiment.

And Tommy stayed put right there in Branch's room.

> "Black skin, black skin. If I could only make 'em white," Tommy kept muttering and rubbing his hands, trying to rub off the blackness. It was a scene that stayed with Branch the rest of his life.

Tommy was there later that night when Branch and the team's captain planned their game strategy. Tommy sat off in a corner all by himself. Hunched over on the end of his cot, the first baseman kept rubbing his two hands, over and over. Tears welled up in his eyes and trickled down his cheeks. His big shoulders heaved. Branch was trying to listen to his team captain, but he could not take his eyes off Tommy.

"Black skin, black skin. If I could only make 'em white," Tommy kept muttering and rubbing his hands, trying to rub off the blackness.

It was a scene that stayed with Branch the rest of his life. It was a scene that started ideas brewing and eventually changed baseball history.

Lawyer, Coach, Speaker, Player, Manager

Over the years, important ideas kept brewing in Branch's brain. It was Branch—Mr. Rickey, as he would be called later—whose brain brewed the idea of baseball's farm system. Under Branch's plan, major league ball clubs could train minor league players for their own teams. Folks called the idea crazy, but that didn't stop Branch. His idea changed how professional baseball works. Now *that* was an important experiment!

It was Branch whose brain brewed blackboard talks, sliding pits, and spring training in Florida. It was even his brain that helped brew the Knothole Gang (special game tickets for kids) and the Fellowship of Christian Athletes. Sports, Branch believed, could help train moral character. The discipline of baseball could make you a better person. He once explained, "A man who is master of himself in other ways will master himself on the mound."

> "A man who is master of himself in other ways will master himself on the mound."

In between all these ideas, Branch was busy following his passions: playing Major League Baseball (with a so-so .239 lifetime batting average); getting married to his sweetheart and raising their five girls and one boy; coaching football, basketball, and baseball; and speaking for causes, especially at the YMCA. (Branch once brought in the great educator Booker T. Washington to speak at his Delaware, Ohio, YMCA.) All this was enough to make anyone tired—even someone like Branch.

And tired he became. One time, he was so worn out that he came down with tuberculosis, an illness he had to take seriously if he was going to be around to enjoy more baseball. Branch wasn't one to sit still, but this time he needed to listen to those who loved him best. It's a good thing he did, too, or baseball might not be the same today.

But it was hard to keep a man like Branch sitting still for long. After a forced rest in the Adirondack Mountains, Branch up and went to law school at the University of Michigan. Not only did he graduate near the top of his class in 1911, but he also coached the baseball team while he was there. He couldn't resist that.

Although Branch thought long and hard about the law, he kept coming back to baseball. Sure, he practiced law for a year in Idaho, but he breathed baseball all year round, wherever he was. Not surprisingly, Branch returned to coach at the University of Michigan. Later, he got a call to manage the St. Louis Browns. He accepted!

Branch playing for the St. Louis Browns, 1906

Over the years, he also worked as vice president of the Browns; as president, field manager, and general manager of the St. Louis Cardinals (with six National League pennants); most famously as president and general manager of the Brooklyn Dodgers (with two pennants); and finally as general manager of the Pittsburgh Pirates.

> "Think a lot, and don't throw away your time. Embrace everything that will be of benefit to you."

You see, Branch liked the way baseball exercised both the body and the mind. He used to say, "Think a lot, and don't throw away your time. Embrace everything that will be of benefit to you."

His name was Branch, and in his brain was brewing a great experiment.

Lots of ideas kept brewing in Branch's brain—too many to even fit in this book. But one of the biggest was the integration of African Americans into Major League Baseball.

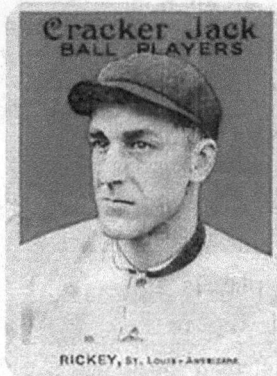

Baseball card of Branch when he was with the St. Louis Browns

5

Theory and Experiment

Now, Branch called it the Great Experiment, and it was *grand*—oh, it was grand! It took everything he'd already learned about patience, courage, and determination. It took standing up for what is right, and most importantly, it took finding the right people to stand up with him. Oh, Branch liked that.

The idea had been brewing in Branch's brain for a good many years—some say ever since he saw Tommy frantically rubbing his hands, mumbling, "Black skin, black skin. If I could only make 'em white." Branch still thought about that moment.

Eventually the thought of Tommy became an idea, a theory, about how to make better baseball and a better world. Branch just needed to find the best people to help prove his hypothesis. The most important fellow scientist in this experiment was the player. Everything depended on him.

In those days, black players and white players weren't allowed to be teammates. It didn't matter how good the player was. Didn't matter how hard he hit. Didn't matter how many runs he got. There were white leagues, and

Branch in the early 1940s

Branch Rickey
Baseball Timeline

1911
Graduated from law school at the University of Michigan

1913
Was manager of the St. Louis Browns, front office

1917–1919
Served in World War I

1919–1942
Was president of the St. Louis Cardinals until 1920
and then manager

1942–1950
Was president and general manager of
the Brooklyn Dodgers

1951–1955
Was general manager of the Pittsburgh Pirates

1957
Started work on President Eisenhower's Committee
on Government Employment Policy

1962
Returned to the St. Louis Cardinals as a
general consultant

1965
Died

then there were the Negro Leagues. The Negro Leagues had no shortage of dynamite players: Satchel Paige, Josh Gibson, Ray Dandridge, "Judy" Johnson, Roy Campanella, Don Newcombe, Larry Doby, and many, many others. Those guys knew their baseball.

By the 1940s, when Branch was with the Brooklyn Dodgers, he knew that to be the very first black player on a team in America would take not only a good player but the absolute best, up-to-the-challenge player imaginable.

Branch also knew that not all of white America was ready for his Great Experiment. That's what made it an experiment. To prove to America that his theory that black and white professional athletes could and should play together, Branch needed to plan his strategy very, very carefully. "Luck," Branch always said, "is the residue of design."

> ## "Luck is the residue of design."

First, Branch went back to his books. The more he read, the more he understood that patience and determination—not violence—were the keys to a successful experiment. One of his favorite books, *Life of Christ* by the Italian writer Giovanni Papini, praised the nonviolent nature of Jesus. Branch studied sociologists and pondered Mohandas Gandhi's practice of active nonviolence. To be successful, this experiment had no room for fistfights. Nope, no more fistfights but lots of fighting without fists. It was going to be a battle. Branch knew that.

Some even called Branch the Mahatma, a respected title given to Gandhi. Others tagged him the Ferocious Gentleman, the Professor of Baseball, the Brain, and the Deacon. Some sneered and questioned his motives, labeling his office the Cave of Winds. But that didn't stop Branch. On a sign hanging in his office were the words, "He who will not reason is a bigot; he who cannot reason is a fool; and he who dares not reason is a slave." Sir William Drummond said that. Branch surely agreed.

His name was Branch, and in his brain was brewing a great experiment.

Branch knew he'd have to choose not only the right person but also the right time and place. In 1943 New York, folks were talking. Integration in baseball was the chatter. Branch chose his strategy carefully and set his sights on Brooklyn. In January, he met with George McLaughlin at the Brooklyn Trust Company to set up the experiment. Branch argued that after World War II, the Dodgers would need more ballplayers. It would make good business sense, he explained, to bring in new, young recruits, who might include a black player or two. There was money to be made. There was a pennant to be won. George McLaughlin nodded. He could see Branch's point. One hurdle cleared for Branch.

Branch kept his longtime plan quiet. He did not raise his famously loud voice while others were forming committees. Make a headliner announcement too early, thought Branch, and—pow, bam—you've got riots. The experiment could go up in smoke before it even got started. Branch couldn't have that. Instead, he kept working in secret with only a handful of confidants.

The plan for his slow-and-steady, hush-hush experiment was simple but difficult:

1. Get the Brooklyn Dodgers's board of directors on his side. This was easier now that the Brooklyn Trust Company had said okay, and the first hurdle was cleared.
2. Sign a terrific ballplayer who could fight the battle for integration—without violence. Only those with tremendous courage need apply.
3. Work hand in hand with local black leaders. Restraint, communication, and coordination would be key.
4. Win over newspaper, magazine, and radio folks. Never underestimate the power of the press!
5. Convince those in the stands (the fans) and those on the field (fellow players).

One of the folks Branch needed to convince was "Red" Barber, the much beloved baseball announcer. Raised in the Deep South, Red was sure he'd have to quit. He just couldn't do his job, he reasoned, with a black man on the team.

Baseball announcer "Red" Barber

Branch knew the fans wouldn't like that. They would not like it at all if Red left. Baseball and Red's voice—they went together! What would Branch do?

"He's coming," Branch confided to Red firmly. But then Branch did something just as important. He waited. He thought Red was a man of reason. Branch gave him time to think. "You can't solve everything in a minute," Branch once said. "Make time your ally. Delay sharp action."

It's a good thing he did. Red went home, talked with his wife, wrestled with his conscience, and decided that, yes, he could report—simply report—the events in the ballpark. Later on, Red knew he'd made the right decision. His decision, and voice, helped persuade others down the line.

6

It's All Up to Jackie

It wouldn't be easy. Branch knew that. All of this would take time, hard work, patience, and courage, plenty of courage. When Branch's scout Clyde Sukeforth brought Jackie Robinson to the Dodgers's New York office, Branch would know soon enough that he had the right man.

Robinson, a shortstop with the Negro League's Kansas City Monarchs and an all-around athlete, had spirit. He was, as Branch liked to say, adventurous. In his years as a second lieutenant in the army from

Jackie Robinson, who, with the help of Branch Rickey, broke the color barrier in baseball and professional sports as a whole in the United States.

1942 to 1944, Jackie had stood up time and again against discrimination. He had even refused to move to the back of an intra-camp bus. Then, when ordered, he refused to leave the bus. He was court-martialed for his actions, and eventually he was honorably discharged.

Yes, Jackie had baseball talent, integrity, and spirit, but—Branch wanted to know—did he have the patience and self-control to win the larger battle and ensure the success of the experiment?

And so, the intense interview of August 28, 1945, began. It lasted a long three hours. Did Jackie have a girlfriend? If she was the right girl, marry her! Branch knew Jackie would need someone to stand by him. They would both need to be very, very courageous.

Did Jackie know why he was there? No, not to play for the Brown Dodgers, a Negro league team. To play for Brooklyn! He would start with the farm team, the Montreal Royals, and then—if he performed well—on to the Dodgers as a major leaguer! "I want to win the pennant, and we need ballplayers!" Branch bellowed, and he slammed his hand on the desk.

Jackie was stunned, but Branch kept right on talking. He waved his cigar in the air. He paced the room.

His name was Branch, and in his brain was brewing a great experiment.

A picture of Branch from a photo spread in LOOK *Magazine, 1946*

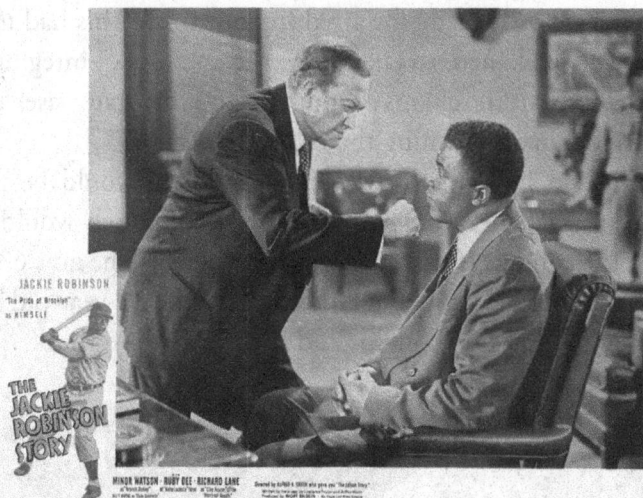

A "lobby card" from the 1950 movie The Jackie Robinson Story.
Jackie played himself, and Branch was played by actor Minor Watson.
In 2013, the movie 42 was made about Jackie Robinson. Harrison
Ford played Branch and Chadwick Boseman played Jackie.

He had even more big questions to ask and buttons to push: Did Jackie have the guts? Not the guts to fight back but the guts *not* to fight back?

Now Branch really went into action. He pretended he was first *this* racist person and then *that* one. He ridiculed, he yelled, he jabbed his fist in Jackie's face. He called him all the names Jackie would be called.

"Get out. No room for you in this hotel, boy," from a hotel clerk.

"Get out. No food for you at this restaurant, boy," from a waiter.

"Get out! No seat for you on my train," from a conductor.

"*Get out!* No game for you at this ballpark," from a spectator.

"*Get out!* No place for you in *our* baseball," from a sportswriter.

And then Branch became a mean-as-they-come bully ballplayer pretending to slam into Jackie with his spikes. "Take that!"

"Could Jackie take it?" Branch needed to know. Could he be more than just a good ballplayer and make the experiment work? It was all up to Jackie.

Now Branch pulled out his much-loved copy of *Life of Christ* and started reading: "Turning the other cheek means not receiving the second blow. It means cutting the chains of the inevitable wrongs at the first link. Your adversary is ready for anything but this." This had to be their way in, Branch explained, to take down the enemies of integration.

Could Jackie cut the chains of injustice and integrate baseball? Could he fight for equality by turning the other cheek?

Could he do it for three whole years? There would be problems. "Problems are the price you pay for progress," Branch would say. Did Jackie have the courage to pay the price for progress? The now 63-year-old general manager of the Brooklyn Dodgers gave the 26-year-old ballplayer a big helping of food for thought, and then he let him think.

"Mr. Rickey, I've got two cheeks."

"Mr. Rickey," Jack Roosevelt Robinson finally answered, "I've got two cheeks." Jackie walked out of that office with a signed contract. And the experiment was on!

7

First Endure, Then Pity, Then Embrace

Many grand and glorious things happened over the next three years, as did many horrific, scary things. Good things like Jackie marrying his sweetheart Rachel, folks celebrating in the streets, and fans of all colors cramming the stands at games—adding up to record attendances. Jackie was a celebrity as big if not bigger than any athlete or rock star today.

But all the joys and celebrations were tainted by taunts, threats, and intimidations. For a while, insults infiltrated the airwaves. Slurs saturated the ballparks. It is much harder to win arguments with fast running than with fast fists. It's much tougher to turn the other cheek than spit back. Good baseball and good character were Jackie's weapons. Boy, did he need them!

All the insults that Branch predicted in August 1945 came true—and then some: pitches straight to the head, spiked shins, hate mail, promises to kidnap Jackie's family, angry marches, and death threats.

Jackie and Rachel needed each other as they played their mighty roles in the Great Experiment. In 1946, soon after their honeymoon, the newlyweds traveled to Daytona Beach for Jackie's spring training. Usually, wives weren't allowed, but Branch knew Jackie would need Rachel. As it turned out, even the trip down was hard, hard, hard. At the New Orleans airport, Rachel faced whites-only bathrooms and water fountains. The airlines bumped the couple from their flight, waiters refused them a seat at the airport coffeehouse, and the Robinsons made do with a shoebox

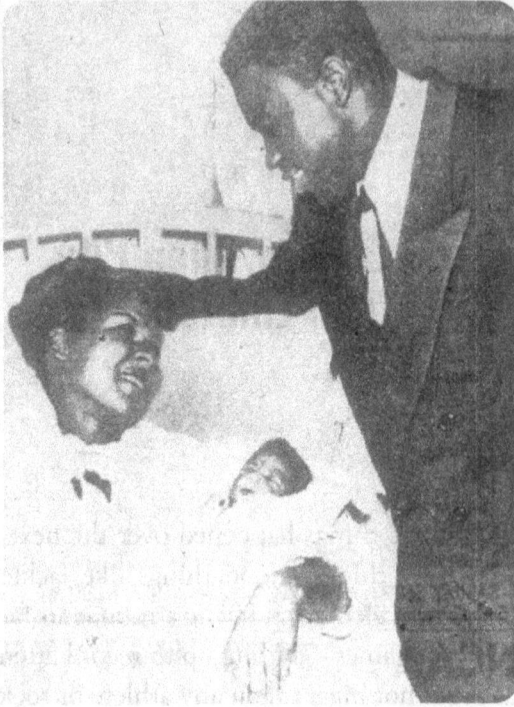

American baseball player Jackie Robinson at the bedside of his wife Rachel, who is holding their newborn daughter Sharon

of food packed by Jackie's mother. Twelve hours later, they finally had a flight out. Rachel and Jackie thought they were on their way.

At the next stop on the plane trip, they were bumped again. Truth be told, their seats were given to white travelers. Resigned to riding the bus the rest of the way, the now-late-to-spring-training Robinsons kept running head-on into Jim Crow—stereotypes and discrimination supported by laws. Some folks didn't know who the Robinsons were. Others did not care. All they saw was black. The great ballplayer and his courageous wife were ordered to sit in the back of the bus. Tired and seething yet in control, they somehow endured sixteen more hours of travel. But there was much more to come.

In the days and years that followed, many folks rallied around Jackie and Rachel. Others did not. Clay Hopper, the Montreal manager, infamously asked, "Mr. Rickey, do you really think [Jackie's] a human being?" This was exactly why they *needed* to succeed. This was exactly why Branch, the Robinsons, and scores of other strong individuals kept marching on.

Many more hurdles were cleared—in Montreal, in Brooklyn, and throughout the United States. But eventually the Great Experiment changed history. Branch knew it could, with the right ballplayer leading the way for others. It was, Branch said, just as the poet Alexander Pope wrote in *An Essay on Man*:

Vice is a monster of so frightful mien,
As to be hated, needs but to be seen;
Yet seen too oft, familiar with her face,
We first endure, then pity, then embrace.

In his Great Experiment, Branch hoped Americans would first endure, then pity, then embrace this African American Rookie of the Year with a strong arm and a courageous heart.

But Branch did not stop. He still had ideas brewing in his brain. There were more players to hire, more baseball games to play, more civil rights speeches to give, and more Jim Crow laws to challenge by setting up exhibition games in the South. He tried to form the Continental League, a third major league (1959–1960), and he published his only book, *The American Diamond* (1965).

In 1962, Jackie was inducted into the National Baseball Hall of Fame. In 1967, Branch's spirit followed. In between, at the Daniel Boone Hotel in Columbia, Missouri, an ailing Branch was inducted into the Missouri Sports Hall of Fame. That night, he spoke on one of his favorite topics: physical and moral courage. Beginning with a well-loved Bible story, Branch suddenly jerked. "I don't believe I can continue," he uttered. Then he slumped over and collapsed.

A few weeks later, on December 9, 1965, the almost 84-year-old visionary died. People from everywhere flocked to pay him homage, remembering, as Branch had said earlier in his life, "It is not the honor that you take with you, but the heritage you leave behind."

Branch's Great Experiment came before Rosa Parks and the Alabama bus boycott. It came before *Brown vs. the Board of Education*. It even came before the integration of the U. S. military. Yet Jackie and Branch shattered baseball's color barrier. It was a Great Experiment indeed.

A Branch Rickey Family Album

Young Branch Rickey

Branch Rickey, 1912, Michigan baseball team portrait

Young Orla Rickey (Branch's older brother)

Orla Rickey

Emily Brown Rickey

Emily Brown Rickey

Frank Rickey and Emily Brown Rickey

Branch's signature

Harold Grimm, Thelma Rickey Grimm, Orla Rickey, Roberta Clark Maddox (the author's mother)

Thelma Rickey Grimm, Roberta Clark Maddox, Marjorie Rickey, Jane Grimm Minton, Orla Rickey, Winnie Rickey, and Frank Rickey

Branch and his wife, Jane Moulton Rickey

Branch Rickey at Orla and Winnie Rickey's home in Bexley, Ohio

Frank and Branch Rickey at Branch's home in Fox Chapel, Pennsylvania

Roberta Clark Maddox with Branch Rickey at his home

Brothers Orla and Branch Rickey

Sue, Betty, Uncle Branch, Aunt Jane, Jane, Mary, Thelma, and Branch Jr.

Branch Rickey between 1909 and 1919

Branch Rickey, St. Louis Browns

RICKEY, Farm System

Branch Rickey baseball card

Jackie Robinson and Branch Rickey signing photo, Associated Press Wirefoto

Pirate player with general manager Branch Rickey

ONLY MAJOR LEAGUE BASEBALL MANAGER
WHO DECLINES TO HANDLE TEAM SUNDAY

BRANCH RICKEY (LEFT) AND BERT SHOTTEN.
The only big league manager who refuses to handle his team Sunday is Branch Rickey of the Cardinals. He never goes to the park on the Sabbath, it being a matter of principle with him to indulge in neither sport nor business on Sunday. During his absence he turns the reins over to Bert Shotten.

Branch Rickey and Burt Shotton, The Boston Globe, *May 12, 1924*

Branch Rickey

Randy Minton, Jane Grimm Minton, Branch Rickey, Marjorie Maddox (the author), Jane Moulton Rickey, Rickey Maddox (the author's brother), Roberta Clark Maddox, at the home of Marjorie Rickey

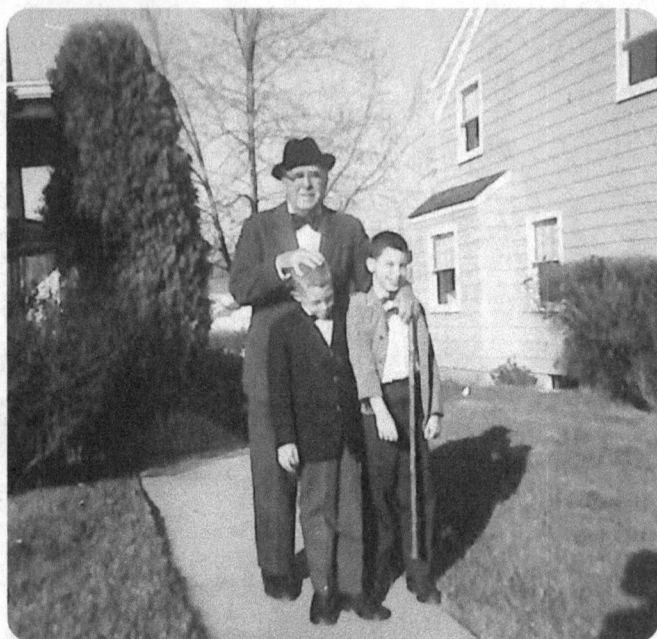

Branch with his great-grandnephews, Randy Minton and Rickey Maddox

Back row: Mary Rickey Eckler (Branch's daughter), Harvey Minton, Jane Grimm Minton, Roberta Clark Maddox; Front row: Marjorie Rickey, Thelma Rickey Grimm, Branch Rickey with Randy Minton on his lap, Jane Moulton Rickey with the author, Marjorie Maddox, on her lap, William (Bill) Maddox (the author's father) with Rickey Maddox on his lap

20' x 40'

Branch Rickey

Branch Rickey, baseball immortal, with inserts in the mural high-lighting some of his greatest achievements during his illustrious career. The mural is bordered to appear as a baseball card.

Promotional calendar for Portsmouth, Ohio, and mural

WESLEY BRANCH RICKEY

ST. LOUIS A. L. 1905-1906-1914
NEW YORK A. L. 1907
FOUNDER OF FARM SYSTEM WHICH HE
DEVELOPED FOR ST. LOUIS CARDINALS
AND BROOKLYN DODGERS. COPIED BY ALL
OTHER MAJOR LEAGUE TEAMS.
SERVED AS EXECUTIVE FOR BROWNS,
CARDINALS, DODGERS AND PIRATES.
BROUGHT JACKIE ROBINSON TO BROOKLYN
IN 1947.

NATIONAL BASEBALL HALL OF FAME & MUSEUM
Cooperstown, New York

Postcard from National Baseball Hall of Fame

Marjorie Maddox with Branch Rickey III at the Baseball Hall of Fame in Cooperstown, New York

Photo Credits

Cover photo: Young Branch Rickey, Branch Rickey family colletction.

Page 4: 1903, Branch Rickey student portrait, Ohio Wesleyan University. Courtesy of Ohio Wesleyan University.

Page 7: 1904, Ohio Wesleyan University baseball team, including Branch Rickey and Charles "Tommy" Thomas. Courtesy of Ohio Wesleyan University.

Page 10: 1906, Branch Rickey playing for the St. Louis Browns. Courtesy of the Library of Congress American Memory, SDN-051982, negatives collection, Chicago History Museum. This image is in the public domain in the United States because its copyright has expired.

Page 11: 1906 baseball card, with the St. Louis Browns. Courtesy of PSA (Professional Sports Authenticator).

Page 12: Branch in the 1940s. Courtesy of Wikimedia Commons. Public Domain.

Page 16: Red Barber at CBS. Courtesy of Wikimedia Commons. Public Domain.

Page 17: Jackie Robinson swinging a bat in Dodgers uniform, 1954. Courtesy of *LOOK Magazine* Photograph Collection, Library of Congress, Prints & Photographs Division, LC-DIG-ppmsc-00047.

Page 18: Branch Rickey, Courtesy of *LOOK Magazine* Photograph Collection, Library of Congress, Prints & Photographs Division, LC-L9-54-7021-A, #15 DLC.

Page 19: Lobby card promoting the movie *The Jackie Robinson Story*, ca.1950. Library of Congress Motion Picture, Broadcasting and Recorded Sound Division. LC-USZC4-6146 (color film copy transparency). Copyright not renewed.

Page 22: Jackie, Rachel and Sharon Robinson, 1950, *Los Angeles Daily News*, unknown photographer. Courtesy of Wikimedia Commons. Public Domain.

Pages. 24–36: Images from the Branch Rickey family collection, courtesy of the author, Marjorie Maddox, great-grandniece of Branch Rickey.

Page 31, top image: Branch Rickey between 1909 and 1919. Courtesy of Wikimedia Commons. Public Domain.

Page 31, middle image: Branch Rickey, St. Louis, AL (baseball), 1913, from the George Grantham Bain collection at the Library of Congress. Courtesy of Wikimedia Commons. Public Domain.

Page 32, bottom image: Pirate player at the Pittsburgh exhibition game chatting with general manager Branch Rickey, April 1955, *Jacksonville Journal*. Courtesy of Wikimedia Commons. Public Domain.

Page 32, top image: Branch Rickey and Burt Shotton, 1924 photo by Underwood & Underwood, *The Boston Globe*. Courtesy of Wikimedia Commons. Public Domain.

Bibliography

Breslin, Jimmy. *Branch Rickey*. Penguin, 2011.

Chalberg, John C. *Rickey & Robinson: The Preacher, the Player, and America's Game*. Davidson, 2000.

Eig, Jonathan. *Opening Day: The Story of Jackie Robinson's First Season*. Simon and Schuster, 2007.

Fox, Stephen. "The Education of Branch Rickey," *Civilization*. September/October 1995: 52-57.

Frommer, Harvey. *Rickey and Robinson: The Men Who Broke Baseball's Color Barrier*. Macmillan, 1982.

Lowenfish, Lee. *Branch Rickey: Baseball's Ferocious Gentleman: with a New Introduction by the Author*. U of Nebraska P, 2009.

Mann, Arthur. *Branch Rickey: American in Action*. Houghton Mifflin, 1957.

Papini, Giovanni. *Life of Christ*. Hamyln, 1957.

Polner, Murray. *Branch Rickey*. Atheneum, 1982.

Posnanski, Joe. *The Soul of Baseball: A Road Trip Through Buck O'Neil's America*. Morrow, 2007.

Rampersad, Arnold. *Jackie Robinson: A Biography*. Knopf, 1997.

Rickey, Branch. *Branch Rickey's Little Blue Book: Wit and Strategy from Baseball's Last Wise Man*. Ed. John J. Monteleone. MacMillan, 1995.

Robinson, Rachel. *Jackie Robinson: An Intimate Portrait*. Abrams, 1996.

United Press International. "On This Day December 10, 1965: Branch Rickey, 83, Dies in Missouri." *The New York Times on the Web Learning Network. New York Times*, 2010.

Acknowledgments

For our many conversations, I am deeply indebted to my mother—who never tired of sharing Uncle Branch tales—to Aunt Jane Rickey Grimm Minton, and to Jenne "Ida Jane" Pugh, Branch's granddaughter and my mother's flower girl. I wish they were present to read this book.

I'm also thankful to my cousin, Jennifer Minton; my sister, Ann Silvey; my brother, Rick Maddox; and my husband, Gary R. Hafer, for help with photographs, as well as for insightful advice and enthusiastic support.

To our children, Anna Lee and Will Hafer, may you carry the narrative forward.

Finally, I am grateful to the good folks at Sunbury Press—especially Lawrence Knorr, Nicole Brown, Crystal Devine, Anaya Montgomery, Darlene Sedjro, and John Jordan—for their help in bringing this important story to younger generations.

About the Author

Marjorie Maddox is the great grand-niece of Branch Rickey, the general manager of the Brooklyn Dodgers, who helped break the color barrier by signing Jackie Robinson to Major League Baseball. The author of *Rules of the Game: Baseball Poems*, she twice has presented at the National Baseball Hall of Fame in Cooperstown, New York, and twice served as official author of the Little League World Series in Williamsport, Pennsylvania, where she and her husband raised their two (now grown) children.

Photo by Melanie Rae Buonavolonta

Professor Emerita of English at the Lock Haven campus of Common-wealth University, she has published 17 collections of poetry—including *How Can I Look It Up When I Don't Know How It's Spelled? Spelling Mnemonics and Grammar Tricks* (Kelsay Books); *Seeing Things* (Wildhouse); and *Hover Here* (Broadstone Books), as well as the ekphrastic collaborations *Small Earthly Space*; *Heart Speaks, Is Spoken For* (both with Karen Elias) and *In the Museum of My Daughter's Mind* (with daughter Anna Lee Hafer, www.hafer.work, and others), a 2023 Royal Dragonfly Book Award in photography/fine arts and American Fiction Award Winner in poetry.

In addition, she has published the story collection *What She Was Saying* (Fomite Press); four children's and YA books—including *Inside Out: Poems on Writing and Reading Poems with Insider Exercises* (Kelsay Books,

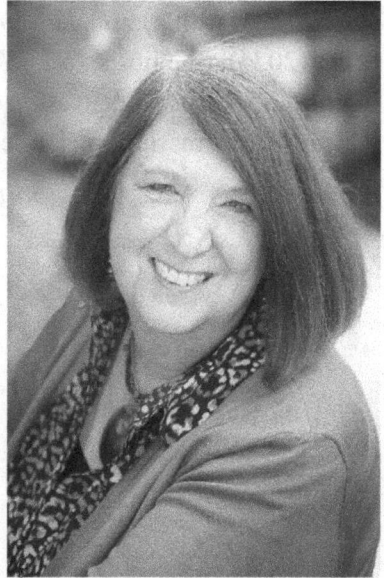

Finalist International Book Awards); *A Crossing of Zebras: Animal Packs in Poetry* (Boyd Mills Press/Wipf & Stock); *I'm Feeling Blue, Too!* (Wipf & Stock, a 2021 NCTE Notable Poetry Book); and the aforementioned *Rules of the Game: Baseball Poems* (Boyd Mills Press/Wipf & Stock).

She is the assistant editor of *Presence: A Journal of Catholic Poetry* and the co-editor, with Jerry Wemple, of two anthologies from Pennsylvania State University Press: *Common Wealth: Contemporary Poets on Pennsylvania* (2005) and *Keystone Poetry: Contemporary Poets on Pennsylvania* (2025). She hosts *Poetry Moment* for WPSU-FM. The recipient of numerous awards, she gives readings and workshops around the world. For more information, please see www.marjoriemaddox.com.

www.ingramcontent.com/pod-product-compliance
Lightning Source LLC
Chambersburg PA
CBHW011802040426
42449CB00016B/3469